CALL OF THE WILD

The Language of Elephants and Other Large Mammals

Megan Kopp

Cavendish Square

New York

Published in 2017 by Cavendish Square Publishing, LLC
243 5th Avenue, Suite 136, New York, NY 10016

Website: cavendishsq.com

This publication represents the opinions and views of the author based on his or her personal experience, knowledge, and research. The information in this book serves as a general guide only. The author and publisher have used their best efforts in preparing this book and disclaim liability rising directly or indirectly from the use and application of this book.

CPSIA Compliance Information: Batch #CS16CSQ

All websites were available and accurate when this book was sent to press.

Library of Congress Cataloging-in-Publication Data

Names: Kopp, Megan, author.
Title: The language of elephants and other large mammals / Megan Kopp.
Description: New York : Cavendish Square Publishing, [2017] | Series: Call of
the wild | Includes bibliographical references and index.
Identifiers: LCCN 2016001077 (print) | LCCN 2016002507 (ebook) |
ISBN 9781502617286 (pbk.) | ISBN 9781502617224 (library bound) |
ISBN 9781502617101 (6 pack) | ISBN 9781502617163 (ebook)
Subjects: LCSH: Animal communication--Juvenile literature. |
Elephants--Vocalization--Juvenile literature. |
Mammals--Vocalization--Juvenile literature. | Animal behavior--Juvenile literature.
Classification: LCC QL737.P98 K635 2017 (print) | LCC QL737.P98 (ebook) | DDC 591.59--dc23
LC record available at http://lccn.loc.gov/2016001077

Editorial Director: David McNamara
Editor: Kelly Spence
Copy Editor: Rebecca Rohan
Art Director: Jeffrey Talbot
Designer: Joseph Macri
Production Assistant: Karol Szymczuk
Photo Research: J8 Media

The photographs in this book are used by permission and through the courtesy of: Hira Punjabi/Lonely Planet Images/Getty Images, cover; Manoj Shah/The Image Bank/Getty Images, 4; Petra Christen/Shutterstock.com; Impalastock/iStockphoto.com; Ishara S.KODIKARA/AFP/Getty Images, 6; Beverly Joubert/National Geographic/Getty Images, 8; Cedric Favero/Moment Open/Getty Images, 11; Michael Leidel/iStock/Thinkstock, 12; Lukas Maverick Greyson/Shutterstock.com, 14; WLDavies/iStockphoto.com, 15; Thomas_Moore/Thomas Moore/iStock/Thinkstock, 16; Johan Swanepoel/Shutterstock.com, 18; EEI_Tony/iStock/Thinkstock.com, 19; Betty4240/iStock/Thinkstock.com, 20; AWEvans/iStockphoto.com, 22; Tom Murphy/National Geographic/Getty Images, 23; kikujungboy/Shutterstock.com, 24; Jerry Alexander/Photographer's Choice/Getty Images, 26, ElephantVoices, 27.

Printed in the United States of America

CONTENTS

Animal Communication

Communication is all about sharing information. One individual sends out a message. Another receives the information. The message can affect the behavior of the receiver.

THIS MEANS THAT

Most humans communicate using spoken words. Animals don't use the same kind of language. They communicate using **signals** or displays. Many animals use sounds to signal other animals. Others use touch. Some use scent. Most animals also use body language to communicate.

4

A mother hippo communicates with her baby using touch and sound.

SPEAKING OUT IN A CROWD

Elephants, giraffes, hippopotamuses, and bison are all **mammals**. This means that they give birth to live young, which feed on milk from their mothers. They are also all **social** animals. They hang out in large groups together.

Sometimes the groups are just mothers and their young. Other times a group is made up of several young males. Groups can also include an entire animal family.

Animals signal one another for many reasons. They need to know when it is time to move and where they are going. Groups need to share if there is danger ahead and

A group of giraffes share information on where to find food. These tall animals eat hundreds of pounds of leaves each day.

where food can be found. Males and females need to find each other to mate. Males communicate to let other males know they are in someone else's **territory**. Mothers need to find their young. Young animals also need to let their mothers know when they need help.

An average herd of elephants has between three and twenty-five members.

When an African elephant bull charges, its flapping ears are a silent sign of aggression.

CHAPTER ONE

Engaging Elephants

Elephants use many calls to express emotion, keep in touch, and pass on information. They rumble, roar, snort, and cry. Some Asian elephants even chirp. Sometimes elephants communicate using **infrasonic** calls. These sounds are too low for humans to hear. These powerful signals travel long distances as **vibrations**.

Elephants have an excellent sense of smell. They use their trunks to track smells on the ground. Elephants regularly touch and smell each other's bodies with their trunks.

BODY LANGUAGE

Elephants send a lot of messages simply by the way they hold their bodies. A frightened elephant might raise its tail and chin. If an elephant quickly flaps its ears and opens its eyes wide, it is excited. At the end of a meal, one family member might go to the edge of the group, lift one leg, and flap its ears. That's the signal to everyone else that it's time to move on. These massive animals also communicate by rubbing their bodies against one another. Sometimes, elephants wind their trunks together to greet one another and show **affection**.

SPECIES STATS

Elephants stand up to 13 feet (4 meters) at the shoulder. They can weigh up to 14,000 pounds (6,350 kilograms). Herds of cows and calves are a common sight. Bulls, or males, are usually **solitary** animals. Elephants are found in Asia and Africa.

Close contact allows a herd of elephants to communicate even when they are on the move.

THE SCIENCE BEHIND VIBRATIONS

Elephants are extremely sensitive to vibrations in the ground. They sense these movements through the soft skin on the pads of their feet. Elephants also lay their trunks on the ground to pick up vibrations. Scientists have observed elephants traveling in a herd freezing in sync to feel these vibrations and process the messages they carry.

Giraffes are the tallest mammals in the world. Their height is useful for keeping an eye out for danger.

CHAPTER TWO

Giraffe Neck Talk

Giraffes seem like the tall, silent type. These animals are generally quiet. They do make sounds when the situation demands it. Females have a long, low-pitched whistle that they use to communicate with their calves. During mating season, males let females know they are in the neighborhood by coughing. Other sounds include hisses and growls.

Scientists recently discovered that giraffes hum to each other. They aren't sure what these messages mean or why these animals hum at night. Some researchers think this is a form of communication.

Like elephants, giraffes use infrasonic calls. These sounds are also used for long-distance communication. A giraffe in the distance might be saying: "Lion coming this way!" Giraffes running away are often early warning signals for other animals that danger is near. When a group of giraffes takes off, other animals follow their lead.

Giraffes can run at speeds up to 35 miles per hour (56 kilometers per hour) for short distances.

A NECK AHEAD

Although giraffes make many sounds, they mostly communicate without sound. Necking is one of the most unique forms of giraffe communication. This is where two male giraffes swing their necks against each other and push. This **dominant** behavior sends a message about which giraffe is boss over the other.

Necking giraffes push against each other to establish dominance.

SPECIES STATS

Newborn giraffes stand about 6 feet (1.8 m) tall when they are born. They grow about 4 feet (1.2 m) before their first birthday. Adults stand about 14 to 19 feet tall (4 to 6 m) and can weigh up to 2,800 pounds (1,270 kg). Giraffes live in Africa. A group of these tall animals is called a herd or a tower.

Hippos hang out in schools of ten to thirty members.

CHAPTER THREE

Hippo Chit Chat

Hippopotamuses love water. They are nicknamed the "river horse." Hippos send signals above and below the water—at the same time. These messages communicate important information, such as the location of other hippos. They also let others know where an individual's territory starts and ends.

Hippos pass on these messages using their **vocal cords**. A hippo makes sounds through its nose, rather than its mouth. Underwater sounds are produced by vibrations in its neck. This way, hippos can communicate above and below water. Hippos aren't quiet animals. They make

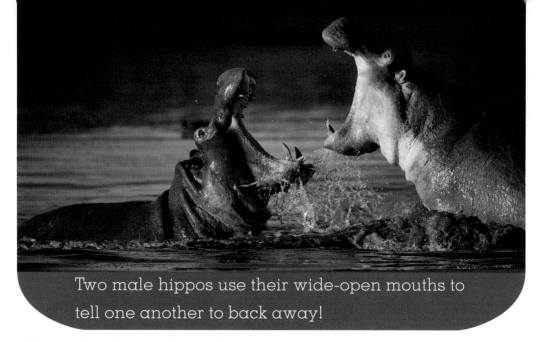

Two male hippos use their wide-open mouths to tell one another to back away!

all kinds of sounds, including bellows, snorts, honks, grumbles, squeaks, and clicks.

LOOKS LIKE A JAW, HEARS LIKE AN EAR!

Hippos spend up to sixteen hours a day submerged in rivers and lakes. This keeps their large bodies cool under the hot sun. Hippos are specially built for life in the water. Their eyes, ears, and **nostrils** are located on the tops of their heads. This allows them to go deep into the water to cool off and still see, hear, and breathe.

A hippo can hold its breath underwater for up to five minutes.

What happens when they go underwater? Ears don't work underwater. So, how do hippos hear messages sent by other hippos? Hippos listen to these sounds through their jaws. There is a thin connection between a hippo's jaw and its skull. This allows vibrations to travel through the jaw and into the ear. There, the vibrations become sounds, which the hippo's brain processes.

SPECIES STATS

Hippos grow up to 14 feet (4.3 m) long and can weigh up to 8,000 pounds (3,629 kg). Hippos are found in Africa. A group of these massive animals is called a school.

Large herds of bison gather during mating season. During the rest of the year, male bison are solitary creatures.

CHAPTER FOUR

Bison Growls, Grunts, and Snorts

Stand and watch a herd of bison in Yellowstone National Park or enjoy a nature documentary about them. You are not likely to walk away thinking these animals are big communicators. It takes time, patience, and plenty of observation to get to know how bison send messages to each other.

BISON SOUNDS

American Bison, sometimes called buffalo, are the largest land animal in North America. They are not the strong,

21

This bull is snorting to warn others to stay away.

silent type. Bison communicate with a variety of sounds. They grunt, snort, and growl. Grunts are used to stay in touch with the herd. Snorts warn intruders to stay away. Bulls may bellow to threaten one another.

SIGNS AND SCENTS

Bison appear much larger when viewed from the side than they do head on. They know it! Bison will turn sideways on purpose to show that they are bigger than another animal. They also send different messages with raised heads and tails.

Smell isn't everything, but it does go a long way in sending signals back and forth when searching for a mate. Both males and females urinate to send messages. During mating season, bulls fight for females by head-butting.

Two male bison face off using their horns.

SPECIES STATS

Standing over 6 feet (1.8 m) tall, bison can weigh up to 2,200 pounds (998 kg). Bison live up to twenty years in the wild. Herds of bison once roamed the open plains of North America. Their territory is now smaller. They can still be found in small herds in grassland parks in Canada and the United States.

Working elephants are a common sight at an elephant camp in Thailand.

CHAPTER FIVE

Bonding with Elephants

In many parts of the world, elephants are working animals. Their intelligence and ability to understand signals from humans allow them to be trained. Elephants and humans have been working together in India for over five thousand years. These mammoth animals carry heavy objects, move timber, and have even been used in battles.

Elephants are used around the world for entertainment in circus shows. Elephants carry tourists on jungle rides in many parts in Asia. While all of these elephants have been tamed, they are still wild animals. Mistreated elephants have been known to attack humans.

How would you interpret this elephant's painting?

On the other hand, elephants never forget those who treat them well. There are many stories of scientists and researchers who have developed close relationships with a particular animal. After years apart, the elephant will still recognize and respond to signals from the human.

Zoo elephants are sometimes given paintbrushes. Their art is a type of communication. There are many **interpretations** of what their paintings might mean.

IN THE FIELD

Scientist Joyce Poole has been studying elephants in Africa for over forty years. She and her husband  started a charity called ElephantVoices. This organization works with education, research, and the **conservation** of elephants.

Thousands of hours of Poole's observations and audio recordings have been organized into online **databases**. They **decode** hundreds of elephant signals and **gestures**. The gesture database covers everything from affection to play and even reactions to death.

Glossary

affection A feeling of fondness or liking.

conservation The preservation and protection of something, like an animal or natural environment.

databases Structured sets of information in a computer that are easily searched.

decode To figure out the meaning of something.

dominant Powerful.

gestures Specific movements that express a meaning.

infrasonic Vocalizations at a frequency too low for humans to hear.

interpretations Explanations for what something means.

mammals Animals that give birth to live young that are fed milk by their mothers.

nostrils Openings in the nose through which air is taken in and pushed out.

signals Sounds or actions used to send messages or warnings.

social Living in groups rather than as individuals.

solitary Being by oneself.

territory An area that is controlled by a group or an individual.

vibrations Movements that can be felt.

vocal cords Folds in an organ in the throat that vibrate and make sound as air passes over them.

Find Out More

Books

Davies, Nicola. *Talk, Talk, Squawk!: How and Why Animals Communicate*. Animal Science. Somerville, MA: Candlewick, 2015.

Lunis, Natalie. *Hippo: River Horse*. Animal Loudmouths. New York: Bearport, 2012.

O'Connell, Caitlin, and Donna M. Jackson. *The Elephant Scientist*. New York: HMH Books for Young Readers, 2011.

Websites

ElephantVoices

www.elephantvoices.org/elephant-communication.html
Visit the ElephantVoices website to learn all about elephant communication.

National Geographic Kids: Giraffes

kids.nationalgeographic.com/animals/giraffe/#giraffe-pair-eating.jpg
Facts, videos, and games about wild giraffes.

Index

About the Author

Megan Kopp is a freelance writer whose passions include science, nature, and the outdoors. She is the author of close to sixty titles for young readers. She loves research and has even gone so far as volunteering to be rescued from a snow cave to get a story about training avalanche rescue dogs. Kopp lives in the foothills of the Canadian Rocky Mountains, where she spends her spare time hiking, camping, and canoeing. She has spent time on safari in Africa watching elephants, hippos, and giraffes.